Christmas decorations (approximately fifty) for trimming the tree and decorating the house or classroom. Many would be fine for gifts. The materials are inexpensive and easy to find.

CHRISTMAS DECORATIONS
for you to make

CHRISTMAS DECORATIONS
for you to make

by SUSAN PURDY

J. B. LIPPINCOTT COMPANY

Philadelphia   New York

Also by Susan Purdy

MY LITTLE CABBAGE
Mon Petit Chou

for
NANCY

DECORATIONS
for your
CHRISTMAS TREE

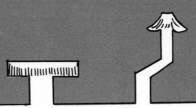

DECORATIONS
for your
HOME

INTRODUCTION

The most beautiful and loved things at Christmas are those you have made yourself. That is what this book is about. You will find that it is divided into two parts. The first part is devoted to decorations for the Christmas tree, the second to decorations for the table, mantlepiece, doorways, and windows of your home or classroom. Many of the projects make lovely gifts for your family or friends.

You will find wide variety among the decorations. Some are quick and easy to make, others take a little more time and patience. Some are old-fashioned, others new and unusual. Imaginative decorations are enjoyed everywhere in the world; several ideas are adapted from decorations of other countries, such as Sweden, Denmark, Italy, and Poland.

Use the suggestions in this book as a starting place for making up your own imaginative designs and decorations. Many of the ideas can be adapted to other holidays. Combine unusual materials, explore, experiment, have fun, and you will have a beautiful holiday.

 **MATERIALS**

The following list consists of *all* the materials used in this book. Each decoration will require the use of only a few at a time. Materials can easily be found in your home, local stationery store, 5 & 10 cent store, craft shop, hardware or department store. If you have any trouble, look in the yellow pages of the phone book.

colored tissue paper
colored construction paper
gift wrapping paper (bits saved from past holidays)
foil-coated gift wrapping paper
extra-heavy colored aluminum foil
colored cellophane
gaily printed wallpaper (wallpaper stores will sometimes give away old sample books)
lightweight cardboard
satin or velveteen ribbon—wide and narrow
trimming—lace, braid, beads, sequins
darning needle
heavy thread
wool
surgical cotton
2-inch styrofoam balls
felt
gold paint (gilt) or gold spray paint
lacquer thinner (removes gilt from brushes)
small paint brush
tempera paint
wax crayons
colored pencils
evergreen branches

mistletoe
wire (heavy and thin)
wirecutters
pipe cleaners
empty coffee can
empty tuna fish can
empty 7-oz. soft drink bottle
empty 6-oz. frozen orange juice can
drinking straws (paper)
paraffin (wax)
flattop pine cones (Red Pine cones are best)
small paper cups (made for hot drinks)
milk cartons
solid-colored Christmas tree balls
small round or oval balloons
straight pins
scissors
ruler
stapler
Scotch or masking tape
cotton string (medium, thick, and thin)
rubber cement (extra rubs off when dry)
Elmer's or Sobo glue (dries clear, don't worry if it shows when wet)
aluminum foil
apron

Before beginning any project, read all the directions through to the end.

Read the instructions on how to trace patterns on the next page.

Use the materials suggested or make up your own variations.

Have fun!

HOW TO TRACE PATTERNS

Always trace patterns, *never* cut book or you will destroy the directions on the other side of the page and will not have the patterns to reuse year after year.

1. Place a piece of tracing paper over the whole pattern· you want to copy. Pull the edges of the tracing paper over the book and *tape them to the table* to hold drawing steady.

2. With pencil, lightly trace the pattern onto tracing paper. (If you press too hard, you will tear through tracing and into the book.)

3. Trace around the outline of the shape. Also, trace dotted lines (which mean *fold*, not cut) and all other markings or numbers within the pattern.

BACK

4. Lift tracing off book and place it *back side up* on scrap paper. With a soft dark pencil, rub all over *back* of tracing. (To transfer onto black paper, rub with white chalk instead of pencil).

FRONT

5. Turn tracing paper *front side up* on top of paper it will be transferred to. Tape down edges of tracing paper. With sharp pencil, slowly and carefully draw over lines of pattern.

6. Compare transferred pattern to original in book to be sure you have traced *all* lines. Pattern is now ready to be cut out.

DECORATIONS
for your
CHRISTMAS TREE

OLD-FASHIONED CHAINS

To make chains, you need a darning needle, thin string or heavy thread, and just about anything you can find to string on the chain. Thread needle and make a knot in one end of your string. Push the needle through whatever object you are stringing, pull object back along the string and add the next piece. If you run out of string, tie a new piece onto the old with a small knot and thread the needle into the new string. When your chain is long enough, tie a knot in the end and hang it on the Christmas tree. (Hang a popcorn chain on a tree outside for the birds' Christmas.)

String popcorn, popcorn, popcorn.

String a cranberry, popcorn, cranberry, popcorn.

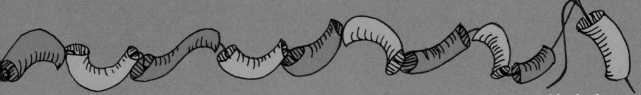

String dry macaroni. To color, dip the macaroni quickly into a bowl of vegetable food coloring and dry before stringing.

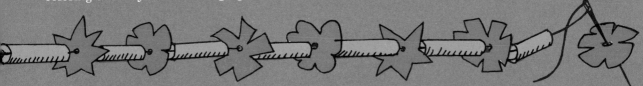

Cut colored plastic drinking straws into short pieces and string with cut colored paper shapes.

Make or buy small Christmas candies wrapped in brightly colored papers. String the papers, letting the candies hang down from the chain.

13

 # POPCORN BALLS

1. To make 14 popcorn balls, measure 10 cups popped corn into a large bowl.

2. With kitchen scissors, cut 10 marshmallows into pieces, or measure 1 cup marshmallow bits.

3. In a saucepan mix:

   ½ cup light corn syrup   10 cut-up marshmallows
   ¼ cup margarine   or 1 cup marshmallow
   1 cup confectioner's sugar   bits
   2 tablespoons water

4. Place saucepan on stove on *low* heat and stir constantly until marshmallows are melted and syrup begins to boil.

5. Remove saucepan from stove.

6. Add to syrup:

   2 teaspoons vanilla extract

   Stir syrup well. For colored popcorn balls, you can add to all or part of the syrup:

   several drops vegetable food coloring

7. For something different, you can add to the popcorn, *not* to the syrup:

   ¾ cup chopped nuts   or   ¾ cup cut-up gum drops

8. Pour syrup over popcorn, tossing well with two big spoons until all popcorn is covered with syrup. Let popcorn cool slightly.

9. To make balls, put a little margarine or salad oil on your hands, dip into popcorn, and roll a small amount into a ball.

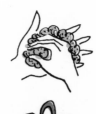

10. Set popcorn balls on waxpaper until hard and no longer sticky, about 1 hour.

11. The popcorn balls may be left plain or wrapped in clear or colored cellophane or foil. Tie with narrow brightly colored ribbon. Make a loop on top of the bow and hang the popcorn ball on the Christmas tree.

CHRISTMAS TREE
BALL SANTA

MATERIALS: White pipe cleaners, scissors, bits of colored paper, glue, solid colored Christmas tree balls and their metal hooks, cotton.

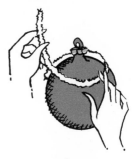

1. Wind a piece of pipe cleaner around the top of the Christmas tree ball. If you are using a large ball, twist 2 pipe cleaners together before winding. Place pipe cleaner 1 inch from top of a medium or large ball, and ½ inch from top of tiny ball. Cut pipe cleaner off at point where ends meet. This will make the border of Santa's hat.

2. Spread a thin line of glue around the ball exactly where you measured the pipe cleaner. Also put glue on one edge of the pipe cleaner itself, and press it onto the ball.

3. Cut out bits of colored paper for the eyes, nose, and moustache. (Moustache can also be made with small rolls of cotton.) Copy shapes on the right but enlarge them as much as necessary. Glue Santa's face onto front of ball, just below border of hat.

4. Take another piece of pipe cleaner and measure the length of a loop from the border of the hat around under the face and back up to the border again. Cut off any extra. Glue pipe cleaner loop onto ball for Santa's beard.

5. Place wire hook in ball and hang Santa on your Christmas tree.

15

TISSUE PAPIER-MÂCHÉ BALL

MATERIALS: Medium-sized round or oval balloon, empty tuna fish can, Elmer's or Sobo glue, water, ribbon or pipe cleaner, string, brightly colored scraps of tissue paper, scissors.

1. Fill empty tuna fish can ⅓ full of glue. Stir in enough water to make glue like heavy cream. If you run out of glue later, make more. Do not add water to what is left, it will be too thin to hold the paper well.

2. Blow up a balloon to the size of an orange. Tie the top with a knot or a piece of string.

3. Tear up *small* scraps of tissue paper. Select the colors of the paper before beginning the papier-mâché. For the brightest, most transparent ball, use light, bright colors. If you put dark colors like brown, dark blue, or green, etc., over bright colors like pink, yellow, or orange, the result will be muddy and dark. Arrange side by side the glue, paper, and balloon.

4. Dip a piece of paper into the glue and smooth it over the balloon. Spread it flat with your finger. Don't worry if the color from the paper runs on your hands (it will wash off) or in the glue (it won't show on the ball when dry).

5. Continue dipping *small* bits of paper into the glue and sticking them onto the balloon. Put each new piece partly over the one already down, so all edges overlap.

6. To be sure there are no air bubbles, always smooth down a new piece of paper until you can see the color of the piece under it. The papers should be wet but *not* soggy. If they get too wet, smooth the surface with your finger, letting the extra glue drip off.

7. Completely cover the balloon with 4—6 layers of paper. Be sure there is no place where you can see the balloon through the paper.

8. Tie a piece of string around the balloon's knot and hang it up to dry. Put newspaper underneath ball to catch the drips.

9. When the papier-mâché is hard enough to hold its shape when tapped, remove string. Tie a ribbon or pipe cleaner into a loop around balloon's knot and hang the ball on the Christmas tree.

STRING WEB BALL

MATERIALS: Medium-sized round or oval balloon, empty tuna fish can, Elmer's or Sobo glue, water, ball of thin cotton string, scissors, narrow, brightly colored ribbon.

1. Fill empty tuna fish can ⅓ full of glue. Stir in enough water to make glue like heavy cream. If you run out of glue later, make more. Do not add water to what is left, it will be too thin to hold string well.

2. Blow up a balloon to the size of an orange. Tie top with a knot or a piece of string.

3. Pull some string loose from the ball. Soak it well in the glue. Wind (do *not* tie) one end around balloon's knot.

4. Hold balloon in one hand, the soaked string in the other, and wind string around the balloon in every direction. Always put the string into the glue, soaking it well, before winding it onto the balloon.

5. Add several layers of string. When you are done, there should be no hole bigger than the size of your little finger nail.

6. To finish, cut the string and loop the end under a piece of the web.

7. Dip your finger into the glue and pat drops of glue all over the string web.

8. Tie a clean piece of string around the balloon's knot and hang it up to dry. Put newspaper underneath ball to catch the drips.

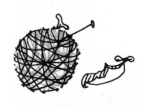

9. Test dryness of balloon in about 3 hours (sooner if drying over heat). Web is dry *only* when stiff and holds shape when gently squeezed. Pop balloon with a pin. (If you pop balloon before web is completely dry, web will collapse.) Pull popped balloon *gently* out through a hole in web.

10. Spray or brush gold paint over the string web. (Be sure it is sitting on scrap paper.) When paint is dry, tie a loop of brightly colored ribbon through web and hang it on the Christmas tree.

 **DANISH CIRCLES**

MATERIALS: Any stiff paper brightly colored on both sides, scissors, heavy thread, darning needle.

Trace patterns. (See page 11.) Transfer patterns to colored paper and cut out.

Bird:
1. With point of scissors, carefully cut line X in side of bird.

2. Cut out wing, slip it through cut in bird's side, and fold wings up in middle.

3. Thread needle, put through top point in circle. Remove needle and tie thread into loop.

Tree:
1. Carefully make cuts on lines X in top and bottom of small tree A. Do *not* cut tree in half.

2. Holding both trees *top up*, slip side of small tree A into cut in circle tree B. Fitting slits of both trees together, push tree A down, then up, to ease it into center of circle tree.

3. Spread out the sides of small tree A so they stand out from the circle and the two trees form a cross.

4. Thread needle, put through top point in circle. Remove needle, tie thread into loop.

5. Make up other designs for inside the circles. Hang them on the Christmas tree or on a mobile (see page 44).

PINE CONE SANTA

MATERIALS: Cotton, construction paper (red, dark and light blue, pink), scissors, glue, thin wire or heavy thread, Red Pine cone (with flattop, about 2½ inches across), 4-inch piece pipe cleaner.

1. Trace patterns. (See page 11.) Note which color each piece should be transferred to. Then transfer and cut out shapes.

2. After cutting out hat, make short cuts into lines around border. Fold on dotted lines bending edges under.

3. Bend hat into cone with folded edges on *inside*. Hold cone together and set on flattop of pine cone to be sure they are same size. If hat is too big, overlap edges more. Mark with pencil where edges meet.

4. When you find correct size, glue hat together at mark, putting glue on inside of one edge and outside of other.

5. Bend pipe cleaner in half, twist stems to make a loop. Cut off very tip of hat. Gently push tips of stems into top of hat. Reach one finger inside hat to spread stems apart.

6. Carefully bend under folded edge of hat to make flat base. Spread glue on base and on flattop of pine cone. Press hat and pine cone together.

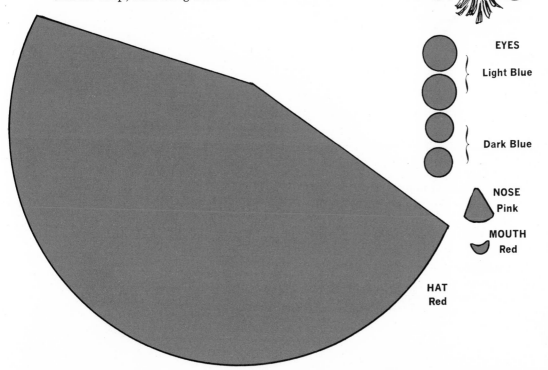

7. While hat is drying on pine cone, glue small dark blue circles onto large light blue circles, making the eyes.

8. Glue eyes and nose onto front of Santa just below the center.

9. For the border of hat, spread glue all around the edge where hat meets pine cone. Press bits of cotton into glue all the way around bottom of hat. Put a drop of glue on the top of hat and add a small ball of cotton. Do *not* hide loop.

10. For eyebrows, carefully drop one dot of glue over each eye and press on tiny pieces of cotton. Roll 2 bits of cotton between your fingers like tiny sausages and glue under nose for moustache. Glue mouth right under moustache, on top of cotton border.

11. Tie a large loop of thread or wire through the pipe cleaner loop, and hang Santa on the Christmas tree.

OR

EYES

Light Blue

Dark Blue

NOSE
Pink

MOUTH
Red

HAT
Red

FOLDED BIRD AND ANGEL

MATERIALS: Stiff construction paper (heavy colored foil for bird, construction paper for angel), darning needle, heavy thread, scissors, colored pencils or paints, and small brush.

Bird:

1. Trace patterns A and B. (See page 11.) To transfer, if you use foil, do *not* scribble over back of tracing. Simply tape tracing onto foil and draw over pattern with sharp pencil. Lines will press into foil. Cut pieces out.

2. Carefully cut into all lines on wings, tail, and head. Curl up all the ends of these strips *except* strips 1 and 2 on wing.

3. Draw bird's eye with pencil. Fold tail *up* on dotted line, toward head. Fold sides *down* on dotted lines.

4. Thread needle. Stitch into the two dots on bird's back, remove needle, and pull thread up into a loop.

5. Cut into line X on bird's wing. Fit this slit X into cut slit X on bird's neck. Hang your bird on the Christmas tree.

Angel:

1. Trace pattern C. (See page 11.) Transfer and cut out pattern.

2. Paint or draw design on face, body, and wings. Make up your own designs or follow this one.

3. Fold wings *back* on dotted lines. Fold base *under*.

4. Thread needle, stitch through top of halo, remove needle, and pull thread up into loop. Hang your angel on the Christmas tree.

24

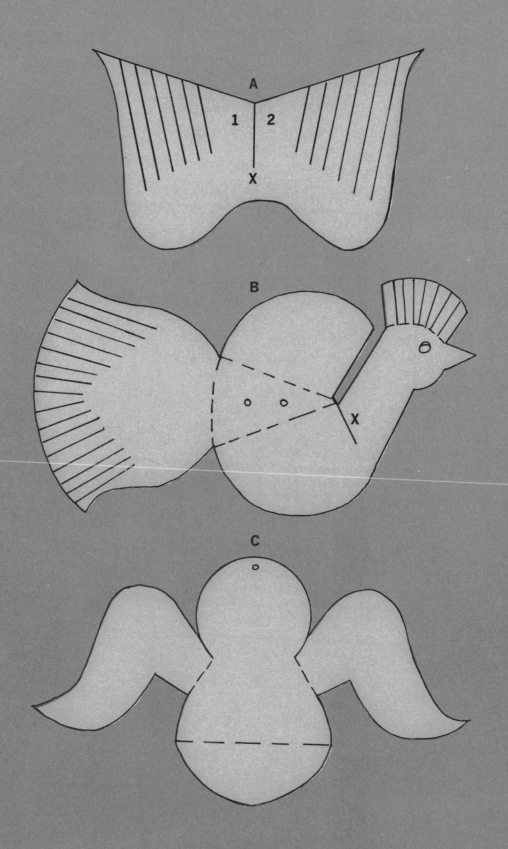

STAINED GLASS

MATERIALS: Black construction paper, colored tissue paper, colored cellophane, crayon, pencil, chalk, scissors, glue, darning needle, heavy black thread, tape.

1. Trace patterns on page 28. (See tracing directions, page 11.) To transfer pattern, *instead* of scribbling on back of tracing with pencil, use white chalk.

2. Fold black paper in half. Be sure *whole* pattern fits over both layers of paper. Tape tracing to top layer and transfer. Hold both layers together and cut shapes out. You should have two pieces exactly alike.

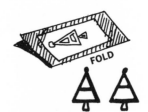

3. Tape one black shape to table. Decide which piece of colored paper you will use first. Place this paper on *top* of black shape and tape down. You can use either tissue or cellophane or a combination of both.

4. You will be able to see through the colored paper. Decide which area you want this color to cover and draw around *outside edge* of it. Draw your shape slightly larger than hole really is. (If you use cellophane, draw on it with crayon.)

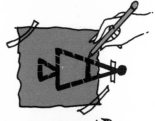

5. Cut out colored paper shape. Do not worry if it is a little big, you will trim it later.

6. Remove tape from black shape, turn it *right side down* on scrap paper and spread glue on edges of that area you will cover first.

7. Glue down colored shape. Smooth wrinkles with your finger.

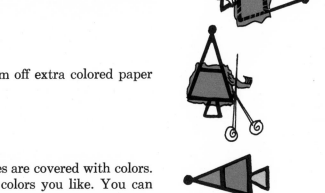

8. Turn black shape over and trim off extra colored paper edges.

9. Repeat steps 3—8 until all holes are covered with colors. Make up any combination of colors you like. You can also design your own black shapes instead of following the patterns.

10. Place second black shape *right side down* on scrap paper. Cover all edges with glue. Turn over, *glue side down* on top of *inside* of first shape.

11. Press pieces together and let them dry well. Trim off edges of colored paper peeking out sides and rub off any glue that shows.

12. Thread darning needle. Put needle through hanging tab of shape. Remove needle and tie thread up into a loop.

13. Hang stained glass shapes on your Christmas tree, in the window, or make several and hang on a mobile (see page 44).

POLISH STAR

MATERIALS: Brightly colored paper, colored tissue paper, glue, scissors, darning needle, heavy thread.

1. Trace patterns on page 31. (See tracing directions, page 11.) Transfer pattern pieces to colored paper. Be sure to transfer pieces C and D to *tissue* paper, and other pieces to a heavier paper. *Cut out 6 pieces of pattern D.* Piece A must be a different color than the 6 circles F. Cut all pieces out.

2. Turn star A *face down* on scrap paper. Spread glue on edges of cut out center circle. Cover with tissue paper circle C.

3. Turn star A *face up.* Glue tiny star G in center of tissue-covered hole, and glue one circle F in the center of each point on star.

4. Fold piece E on dotted lines. Cut all the little lines *just up to the fold.*

5. Turn star B *face down* on scrap paper. Bend strip E into ring around the cutout circle. Fold bottom row of fringe *under and away from center.* When ring is same size as circle, mark the side and glue ends together at this point.

6. With star B still face down, spread glue on edges of cutout center. Also spread glue on top layer of bent-over fringe. Turn the ring *glue side down* onto the circle and press. Be sure all pieces of fringe are well glued to the star.

7. Now spread glue on top layer of bent-over fringe.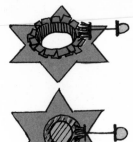

8. Turn star A *face down*, spread glue around edges of tissue circle.

9. Turn star A *face up* and place it on top of glued fringe ring. *Points of both stars should match exactly.* You should *not* be able to see fringe ring through the tissue covered circle.

10. Carefully fold each of the 6 tissue strips D on the dotted line. Make three short cuts along the 3 inside lines. Do not cut too far.

11. Pinch each folded strip together at the base, making the loops open out.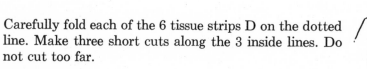

12. Put a drop of glue on inside tips of each point of stars A and B. Press ends of tissue loops onto glue and pinch tips of stars together, catching bottoms of the loops inside.

13. Thread needle and stitch through top point of star. Remove needle, tie thread up into loop and hang your star in front of a window so light can shine through the tissue center. You can also hang the star on the Christmas tree.

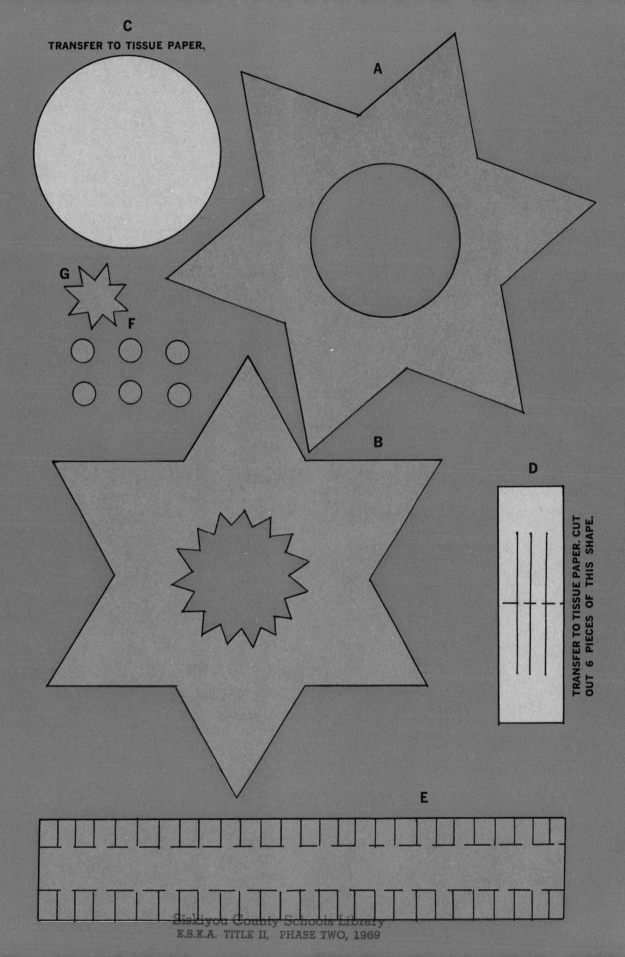

C
TRANSFER TO TISSUE PAPER.

A

G

F

B

D

TRANSFER TO TISSUE PAPER. CUT
OUT 6 PIECES OF THIS SHAPE.

E

SWEDISH STAR

MATERIALS: 10 paper drinking straws, thin red or white cotton string—20 pieces 6 inches long, 2 pieces 12 inches long—scissors, ruler, ribbon, gold paint or spray. (In Sweden the stars are made of real straw reeds and tied with red string.)

1. To measure and cut strings: loop at correct length against side of ruler. When you have enough length, hold all loops together, cut off extra, and cut into each loop at top and bottom.

2. Bend each straw in half.

3. To make first half of the star, take 5 of the bent straws and arrange flat on the table, fitting their "V's" into each other.

4. Holding straws flat, pinch their centers together. While pinching, lift all straws at once and slip a 12-inch string under their centers. Tie string tightly around centers. Spread out arms of star.

5. Repeat steps 3 and 4 to make second half of star.

6. Place one half of star exactly on top of the other. Tie them together in center with the ends of the long string. Wrap the string around both centers several times before knotting. Cut off extra string.

7. Spread all the arms out evenly, matching those of the top star *directly* over those of the bottom.

8. Hold one pair of straws (one is from top, one from bottom star). With a short piece of string, tie the arms together about one inch from the center of the star. Pull string tight and tie a double knot.

9. Take *next* pair of straws and tie as in step 8. *Tie all straws exactly same distance from center of star.* Repeat all the way around.

10. There should now be a circle of the tied straws. The ends of each pair are free.

11. Tie the tip of a straw from one pair to the tip of a straw from the *next* pair in line. For example, tie tip B to tip C, and tip D to E. Continue around whole star this way. Tie tip F to G, H to I, etc. It doesn't matter if the tips that go together are both from top or bottom star.

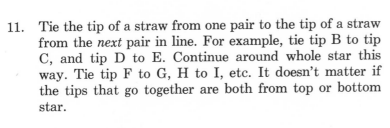

12. When finished you should have a 10-pointed star. Cut off extra bits of string.

13. The star can be left plain, or you can brush or spray on 2 coats of gold paint. When dry, tie a brightly colored ribbon into a loop on top of the star and hang on the Christmas tree. Or, make several stars, with loops of thread instead of ribbon, and hang on a mobile (see page 44).

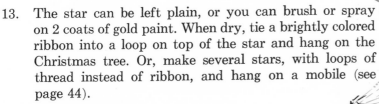

DECORATIONS
for your
HOME

DOORKNOB DECORATIONS

MATERIALS: Colored paper (or you can use felt, but if you do, make a cardboard pattern to draw around), scissors, glue, trimming such as ribbons, braid, beads, bells, etc., pencil.

1. Read tracing directions, page 11. Trace around *outside* edge of the red shape on preceding page. For second piece of pattern, trace around *outside* edge of green shape. Transfer each shape to a different color paper. Cut shapes out.

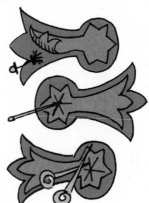

2. Glue smaller shape on top of larger.

3. With pencil, lightly draw 3 cross lines on smaller shape within circle.

4. With point of scissors, cut on these lines. Cut *only* to edge of smaller shape, *not* into outer circle.

5. Decorate streamers with trimming such as beads, ribbons, bells sewn on tips, etc.

6. Press cut star gently over doorknob.

7. Push paper back until it sits *behind* the doorknob.

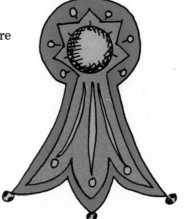

8. Make a doorknob decoration for each room. Here are some other suggestions:

 # CHRISTMAS WREATH

MATERIALS: 7 feet heavy wire (for a wreath 12 inches across), thin wire, scissors, wirecutters, evergreen branches, red ribbon.

1. Wind the heavy wire into a circle about 12 inches across. *Be careful to keep the loose ends of wire away from your eyes.* Double the wire a second time around and wrap the ends over the circle to finish. This is the frame for the wreath.

2. Break small twigs off the evergreen branches.

3. Hold two twigs together and twist a piece of thin wire around their stems. Leave about 3 inches of wire hanging.

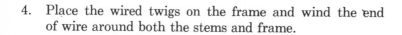

4. Place the wired twigs on the frame and wind the end of wire around both the stems and frame.

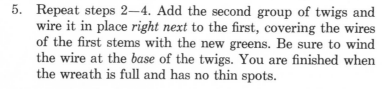

5. Repeat steps 2—4. Add the second group of twigs and wire it in place *right next* to the first, covering the wires of the first stems with the new greens. Be sure to wind the wire at the *base* of the twigs. You are finished when the wreath is full and has no thin spots.

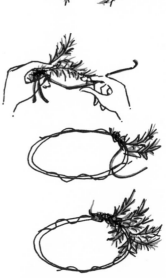

6. The back of the wreath should be smooth. If there are any wires sticking out, twist them into the frame.

7. Tie a bright bow onto the top of the wreath. Tie on colored balls, pine cones, or berries and hang the wreath on the door.

CANDLESTICK WREATH

Use same materials as Christmas wreath.

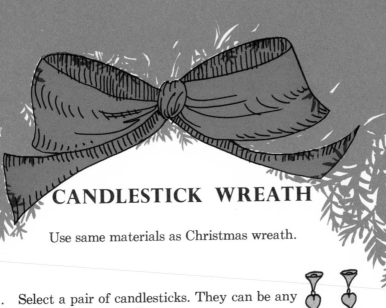

1. Select a pair of candlesticks. They can be any shape, large or small.

2. Wind the heavy wire in a circle around the widest part of the candlestick to find the size and shape of your frame.

3. Double the wire a second time around the circle, and cut the end with wirecutters. Wrap the ends over the circle to finish the frame. Repeat steps 2 and 3 to make the second frame.

4. Follow steps 2—6 of the Christmas wreath directions of preceding page until you have made two miniature wreaths.

5. You can leave the greens plain or tie on tiny colored balls, pine cones, berries, or ribbons.

6. To decorate the holiday table, fit the finished wreaths over the candlesticks and add brightly colored candles.

BOTTLE REINDEER

MATERIALS: Empty soft drink bottle (7-oz. size for pattern), gold paint or gold spray paint, brush, lacquer thinner, colored foil (extra stiff) or construction paper, beads, pearls, or seeds, scissors, glue.

1. Trace pattern. (See page 11.) To transfer pattern if you use *foil paper*, do *not* scribble over back of tracing. Simply tape tracing on foil and draw over pattern with sharp pencil. The lines will press into the foil. If you use construction paper, follow regular transferring directions. Cut shapes out.

2. Paint or spray bottle gold. Be sure to have scrap paper under and around bottle. Let bottle dry.

3. Fold down head on dotted line A. Fold back tip of line B, leaving antlers sticking up.

4. Spread glue on top of bottle and on *under* side of head, between folds A and B.

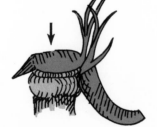

5. Press head, *glue side down*, onto bottle top.

6. Spread a narrow line of glue down center back of bottle. Press tail C onto glue, beginning at very top of bottle. Bend tail *up* on dotted line.

7. Glue paws on front of bottle.

8. For eyes, glue on seeds, beads, tiny pearls, or bits of paper. Glue on a loop of ribbon or bit of paper for nose.

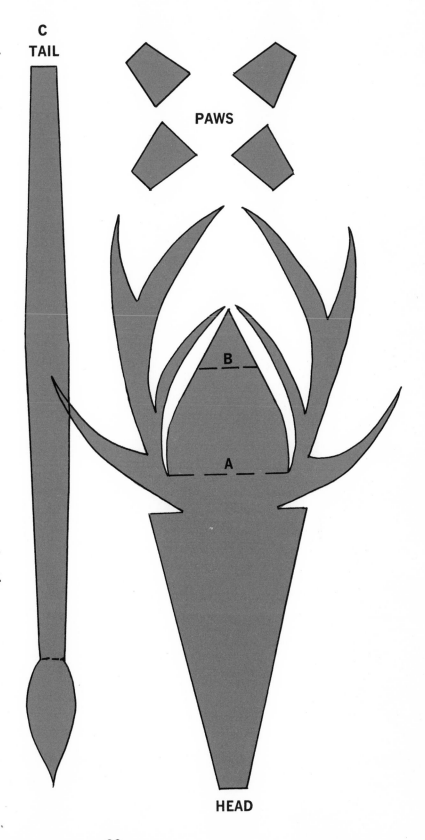

C
TAIL

PAWS

B

A

HEAD

39

ORANGE JUICE CAN SANTA

MATERIALS: An empty 6-oz. frozen orange juice can, colored paper, glue, scissors, cotton, aluminum foil.

1. Trace patterns. (See page 11.) *Before you transfer pieces,* be sure to read on the pattern which *color* each piece should be. Cut pieces out.

2. Spread glue all over the outside of can. Spread glue on under side of piece A, and wrap it—*glued side down*—around the can.

3. For belt buckle, glue pieces C and D onto B.

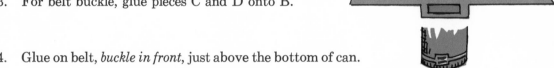

4. Glue on belt, *buckle in front*, just above the bottom of can.

5. For eyes, glue smaller circles onto larger.

6. Above belt buckle, glue on pieces F (beard), and E (hair), then eyes and nose. Rest nose on top of beard.

7. Bend piece G (hat) into a cone. Hold the sides together and set it on top of the can to be sure it fits. Mark where the edges overlap and glue them together up to the mark.

8. Put a drop of glue on top of cone. Stick small ball of cotton onto glue for top knot. Spread glue all around bottom edge of hat and stick pieces of cotton into glue for border.

9. Line the can with foil, fill Santa's belly with candies, and put his hat back on. Or, leave off the hat, tuck a napkin into the can (leave the napkin partly sticking up) and Santa is a gay napkin holder for your Christmas table. For a party, make a napkin Santa for each guest.

40

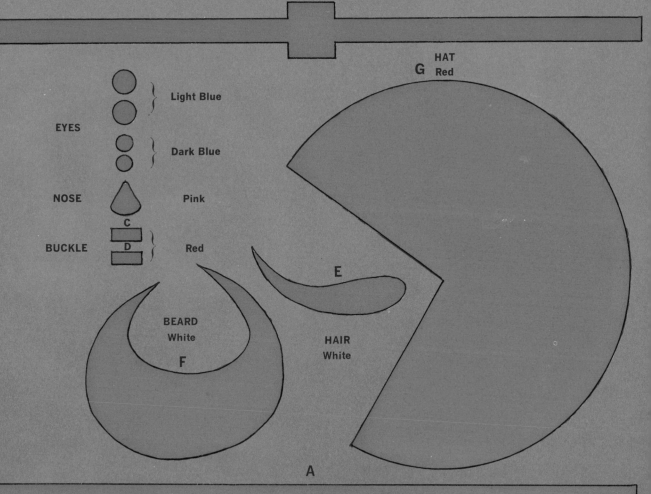

B

EYES

Light Blue

Dark Blue

NOSE
Pink

C
D
BUCKLE
Red

BEARD
White
F

NOSE

E

HAIR
White

G HAT
Red

A

SMALL PAPER ANGEL

MATERIALS: Any stiff colored paper (foil, construction paper, wrapping paper, or wallpaper), scissors, glue, colored pencils or crayons, tape, darning needle, heavy thread.

1. Trace pattern. (See page 11.) Transfer piece D (gown) to a patterned paper. Transfer other pieces to solid colored paper. Cut shapes out.

2. Place piece D (gown) right-side *down* on scrap paper. Spread glue on the inside of one edge, the outside of the other, and pull the edges around into a cone. Press together.

3. Cut off the very tip of the cone, making an opening wide enough to stick in the long neck piece of head (A).

4. Draw the face. Follow pattern or make up your own expression.

5. Cut center out of halo (C) with point of scissors.

6. Hold halo and head pieces together and fit their stems down into the top of gown. Push head down until chin rests on top of gown. Fold halo over top of head.

FRONT   BACK

7. When halo and head are in place, hold them together, tip angel over, and tape both stems to inside of gown.

8. Put a drop of glue on center back of angel. Also put drop of glue on center X of wings. Press wings onto glued center back.

9. Thread needle, stitch through top back of gown, remove needle, and tie thread up into a loop.

10. Hang your angel on the Christmas tree or make several and hang on a mobile (see directions on next page).

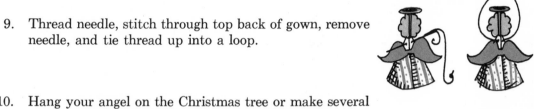

A

B

X

C

D

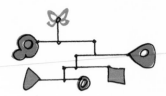

MOBILES

MATERIALS: Mobiles can be made of practically anything: pencils, sticks, drinking straws, thin metal rods, wooden dowels, stiff wire, etc. (If you use stiff wire, you need pliers to make loops connecting the mobile's arms.) Also, you need thin wire, or heavy thread, scissors, and a ruler.

About Mobiles:

The word "mobile" means movable. Mobile sculptures are exciting because they change constantly, moving in the wind. Mobiles were invented by the sculptor Alexander Calder, whose work you can see in many art museums and in art books in the library. There are many decorations in this book that you can hang on your mobiles. Try the stained glass designs, Swedish stars, string web balls, Danish circles, and Polish star. For our example, we will use the small paper angel from page 42.

1. To make this very simple mobile, we will use drinking straws. Measure and mark the first straw to find its center. This straw will be the top of the mobile.

2. Cut a piece of heavy thread about 9 inches long. Tie one end around the center mark of the straw.

3. Take a second straw, cut 2 inches shorter than first, and measure and mark its center. Tie the other end of the thread around this straw's center. The straws should be about 5 inches apart. (Change the length of your thread, distance apart, and position of arms depending on size and shape of decorations to be added.)

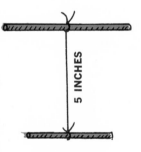

5 INCHES

4. Your straws should *balance*. Balance is the most important part of the mobile. Remember, when you do something to one side, you must then do something to the other to make the mobile balance again. Although you may have measured the centers of the straws correctly, their weights may change the balance. Hold up your straws (or hang them from a hook) and see if they balance. If they don't, move the thread slightly about the centers of straws to adjust.

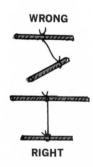

WRONG

RIGHT

5. Thread darning needle and put it through top back of angel. Remove the needle, pull thread through so one end is shorter and tie this end around longer piece. Make double knot. Or instead, tape thread inside gown and pull a length out hole in neck.

6. With the long thread, tie the first angel to one end of the top straw. Let her hang down about 2 inches (just so she does not hit second straw). Tie a second angel, also hanging down 2 inches, in same position on *other* end of top straw. Tie 2 angels on the bottom straw and add an extra angel, hanging down lower, in the center. Adjust the balance of the angels by moving their strings as in step 4. Tie a bow on the center of top straw and hang up your mobile.

7. Experiment with the design of your mobiles, adding more arms in different positions. Remember—when you add to one side, add also to the other, making the mobile balance. Be sure to consider the shape, size, and length of string of the object you are adding. The forms should move *freely*, not banging into each other.

45

FOIL ANGEL

MATERIALS: One styrofoam ball 2 inches in diameter, extra-heavy colored foil, 2 feet yellow or gold ribbon ½ inch wide, trimming (gold braid or edging, ribbon, laces, etc.), tempera or gold paint, small brush, lacquer thinner, straight pins, scissors, glue.

1. Paint face on front of styrofoam ball. See pattern on next page.

2. Read tracing directions, page 11. Tape together two pieces of tracing paper in order to cover all of gown pattern. Trace outline *and* numbered lines on gown. Trace hand and wing outlines. Do not be confused by overlapping lines; each piece should be separate and whole on your tracing.

3. Unroll colored foil and flatten it with your hand. To transfer patterns, do *not* scribble over back of tracing. Simply tape tracing on foil and draw over pattern with a sharp pencil. Transfer gown first, then, for hands and wings, fold the foil *double, right* or prettiest colored *sides together.* Be sure whole patterns fit over *both* layers. Tape tracings down on top layer and draw around them. The lines will press into the foil.

4. Cut out together both hands and both wings. Cut out gown. Be careful not to cut any tabs off. Flatten any wrinkles or bends in foil with your fingers.

5. With point of scissors, cut into slits 1, 2, 3, 4, and 5 in gown.

6. Bend gown around into a cone with point at top. Fold edge with tabs over and slip tabs into slits 1 and 2. On the *inside, bend tabs back* to fasten gown. To smooth cone, rest it in one hand and press foil against palm with the fingers of the other hand.

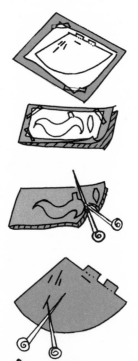

7. Cut the 2-foot strip of ribbon into 8 pieces 3 inches long. Fringe one end of each piece. Glue first 2 strips, fringe down, on either side of face. Continue gluing strips around ball for hair. To finish, glue 2 fringed edges just over eyes and let ends of these strips fall back, covering the other glued ends.

8. Cut a piece of lace or ribbon about 5 inches long and bend it into a ring. Push 2 pins through the ring and into angel's head to fasten the crown.

9. Turn head upside down. Stick point of pencil into center of bottom, turning it a few times to make a hole big enough to sit on the point of the cone.

10. Put a drop of glue inside the hole in ball. Spread glue around the tip of cone, and sit ball on top. Press ball *very gently* to make it stick. If foil tip crushes down, poke it out from inside with pencil point. Add more glue and try again.

11. Add trimming to gown. Bend a piece of ribbon or lace 2½ inches long around the neck, just under head. Fasten by sticking a straight pin through the edges of lace and into foil gown. (Support foil from inside with fingers while sticking pins in.) Glue streamers of ribbon or braid about 8 inches long onto front of gown. Glue on stars, sequins, beads, pearls, etc.

12. Insert wing tabs into back slits 3 and 4. *Longest points* of *both wings* should be *up*, as shown. Fasten wings *inside* cone by bending tabs to the *side, away* from center.

13. Gently bend wing tips down toward the front of the angel. Bend foil until wings hold position. Glue hands pointing upward on wing tips. If necessary, put a drop of glue under wrists to hold them to gown.

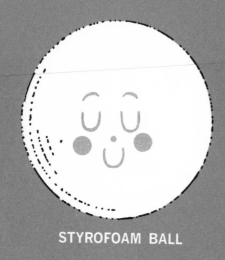

STYROFOAM BALL

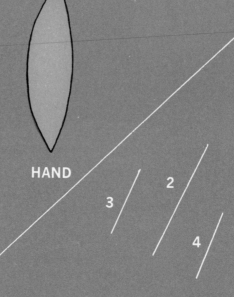

HAND

3

2

4

1

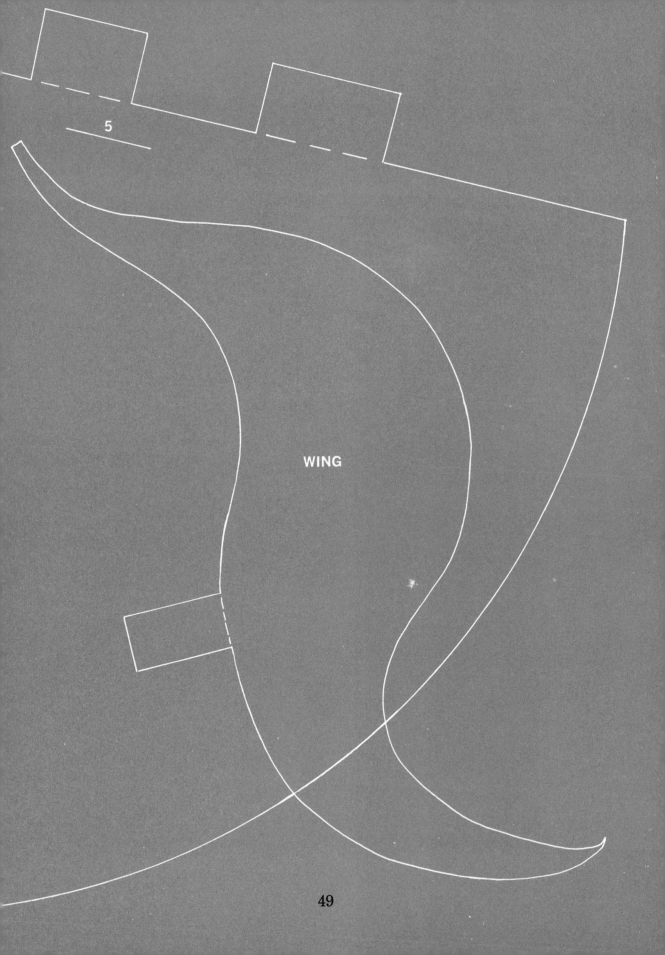

5

WING

49

 **ITALIAN TREE CHAIN**

MATERIALS: Colored tissue paper (contrasting colors such as red and green are especially gay), lightweight cardboard or any stiff paper, thin string, darning needle, scissors, glue (Elmer's or Sobo).

1. Read tracing directions, page 11. Trace tree pattern A from page 53. Fold a piece of cardboard in half, making sure that the whole pattern fits over *both* layers. Tape tracing to top layer and transfer drawing. Hold both sides together and cut out. You should have two cardboard trees exactly alike.

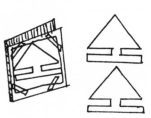

2. Fold a large piece of *red* tissue paper so that you have 6 even layers (or stack 6 sheets together). Be sure there are no short ends and the *entire* cardboard tree fits on top of *every* layer.

3. Hold one cardboard tree down carefully on top layer of the stack and draw around it. Remove cardboard. Holding the sheets tightly together, cut a big circle roughly around outside edge of tracing to get rid of extra paper. This makes it easier to cut out trees.

4. Holding all sheets tightly together, cut carefully around drawing. Try not to let the papers slide. You should have 6 trees exactly alike.

5. Repeat steps 2, 3, and 4 to make *another* 6 red trees. You now have 12 *red* trees.

6. Now make 12 *green* trees, following steps 2, 3, 4, and 5 using *green* tissue paper.

7. Place both cardboard trees flat on the table on scrap paper. Cover them with glue and press one *red* tissue tree over each. Smooth any wrinkles.

8. To glue the chain, use either a glue brush or the tip of your glue container. Stack the red and green trees side by side.

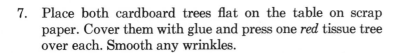

  a. Place one cardboard tree—*tissue side up*—on the table.

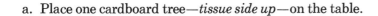

  b. Put a narrow line of glue down the center of this *red* tree.

  c. Place a *green* tree on top of the red and smooth along the glued center line. The green tree is correctly placed if you *cannot* see any red peeking out the edges.

  d. Put one tiny drop of glue at each X on the *green* tree (see drawing).

  e. Place a *red* tree exactly over the green, pressing on the glued points.

  f. Be sure the glue does not leak onto any other parts of the tree or the chain will not open. Wipe off any extra glue while soft.

g. Repeat steps b, c, d, and e until you have used up all the tissue trees. You will notice that you have alternated the colors (red, green, red, green) as well as the places in which the trees are glued. When you reach the last green tree, glue the second red cardboard tree onto it—*tissue side down*—as if it were a regular tissue tree.

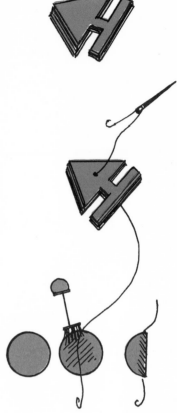

9. You now have a tree sandwich. Cut a piece of string about 2 feet long and thread it through the darning needle. Hold the "sandwich" in one hand and poke the needle through the center of the tree. (See drawing.) If you have trouble getting the needle through, place the "sandwich" on an old magazine and push down on the needle until it goes through the cardboard and into the magazine. Pull the string through the hole, leaving the ends sticking out on each side.

10. Cut 2 small circles of construction paper. Cover one side of each circle with glue, place an end of the string on each, and fold in half over the string. These tabs will keep the string from slipping through the chain.

11. Open your chain very slowly and carefully. Handle the tissue paper gently or it will tear. If it does, repair with Scotch tape. To hang, open chain, pull string taut, tape ends of string onto backs of cardboard trees. The opened chain should look like this:

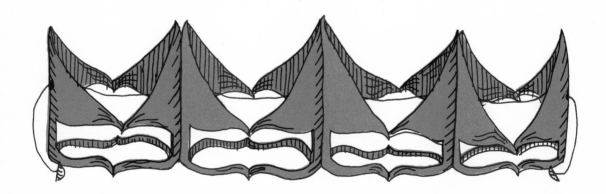

ITALIAN
FLOWER CHAIN

MATERIALS: Same as Italian Tree Chain, page 50.

1. Read tracing directions, page 11. Trace patterns B and C from preceding page. Fold a piece of lightweight cardboard (or any stiff paper) double, tape tracing B to top layer, and transfer drawing. Hold both layers together and cut pattern out. You should have two cardboard flowers exactly alike. Cut circle C from *one* layer of cardboard.

2. Choose two colors of tissue paper that go well together, for example, green and yellow. Fold a large piece of *green* tissue paper so that you have 6 even layers (or stack 6 sheets together). Be sure that there are no short ends and that the *entire* flower pattern will fit on top of *every* layer.

3. Hold *one* carboard flower down carefully on the top layer of the stack and draw around it. Cut a big circle roughly around the outside edge of the tracing to get rid of extra paper and make it easier to cut the flower.

4. Holding all the sheets tightly together, cut around the drawing. Try not to let the papers slide. You should have 6 flowers exactly alike.

5. Repeat steps 2, 3, and 4 to make 6 *more* flowers, 12 in all. This will make a chain about 16 inches long when opened. If you want a longer chain, make more flowers—24 will give you a 32-inch long chain.

6. To make the centers for the flowers, fold a large piece of *yellow* tissue paper so that you have 6 layers (or stack 6 sheets together). Draw around the cardboard circle C and cut out, following steps 2, 3, 4, and 5 above. Then repeat the steps, cutting out as many circles as you have flowers.

7. Glue a yellow center onto each green flower.

8. To cover the cardboard flowers with tissue, place both cardboard flowers flat on the table. Put glue all over one side of one cardboard flower. Before gluing tissue flower down, hold it directly above the cardboard flower and line up their petals. Then press tissue down onto glue and smooth wrinkles. Repeat to cover second cardboard flower.

9. To glue the chain, use either a glue brush or the tip of your glue container.

    a. Place one cardboard flower—*tissue side up*—on scrap paper on table.

    b. Put a *narrow* line of glue down the center of the flower.

    c. Place a second tissue flower—*yellow center down*—on top of the first. You are putting the flowers' centers together. Press along glued line.

    d. The back of the second flower is now up. Put *tiny* drops of glue at points X (see drawing) on petals.

    e. Add next flower—*center up* (backs together)—and press on glued points.

    f. Be careful the glue does not leak onto any other parts of the flower or the chain will not open. Wipe off any extra glue while soft.

    g. Repeat steps b, c, d, e, and f until you use up all the flowers. *Remember*, you are always placing flowers back to back or center to center, lining up petals over each other exactly.

    h. When you reach the last tissue flower, glue the second cardboard flower—*tissue side down*—to the chain as if it were a regular tissue flower.

10. You now have a flower sandwich. To complete the chain, follow steps 9, 10, 11 for Italian Tree Chain, page 52. Your opened chain should look like drawing on right.

CHRISTMAS CANDLES

CANDLEMAKING REQUIRES BOTH THE USE OF THE STOVE AND THE HANDLING OF HOT WAX AND SHOULD BE DONE ONLY WITH THE HELP OF AN ADULT. *Note:* PARAFFIN OR WAX IS INFLAMMABLE IF OVERHEATED OR EXPOSED TO OPEN FLAME.

MATERIALS: Wax—household paraffin or old candle stubs; wicking—medium thick cotton string (or special candle wicking found in hobby shops); molds—glasses or glass jars, cans, (all molds *must* have straight sides *or* top larger than bottom), hot drink paper cups, and milk cartons; coloring—wax crayons (paper peeled off); cardboard; scissors; double boiler (or coffee can set in pan of water); soup ladle; salad oil; apron.

NOTE: Use a double boiler or a coffee can in a pan of hot water, pinching the sides of the can to make a pouring spout. Never melt wax directly over heat or it will splatter.

If you use a can for your mold, be sure to grease it with salad oil before adding wax. You do *not* have to grease glass or paper molds.

If wax spills, hot water will melt and wash it off any surface. Wax on cloth can be removed by ironing cloth between sheets of paper toweling.

Wicks:

To prepare cotton string for wicking, cut a long length of string and dip it in melted wax. Stretch it out and let harden. Cut whatever length you need for your mold and put in wickholder. This is a device to make wick stand up in the center of the candle.

1. Wickholders bought in a hobby shop look like this:

2. You can make your own wickholders:

   a. Tie the end of the wick around a folded up piece of tinfoil or around a penny. This goes in bottom of mold.

   b. Cut a strip of cardboard long enough to lay across top of your mold. Make a hole in the center of strip and pull wick through. You do not need a knot on top.

   c. Drop bottom holder down into center of mold. Rest strip across top. Be sure wick is straight between.

3. Instead of wicking, you can use old candle stubs or birthday candles as ready-made wicks. Stick the whole stub into the *center* of your mold when the wax just begins to cool. (Be sure the stub is as tall as your mold.) You are using the old candle as the core of your new one.

PLAIN CANDLES

Read all direction on page 56.

1. If you are using a milk carton mold, cut it to the height you want. To seal any cracks, pour a small amount of melted wax into the mold, spreading it over bottom and sides. Pour out extra wax and let sealer harden. Grease inside *only* if mold is a tin can.

2. Melt several bars of wax in double boiler. To color, add wax crayons (paper peeled off!) to melted wax. To test color, put a drop of melted wax on a plate and let cool. If too light, add more crayons.

3. Put wick in place in mold and pour in melted wax.

4. Wait about 2 hours, test wax with finger to see if it is hard. When thoroughly hard, remove top wickholder. Cut off wick about 1 inch from candle top. Bottom wickholder stays *in* candle.

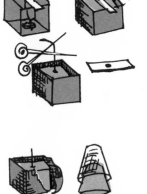

5. To remove candle from mold:
   paper cup or milk carton—peel off paper;
   glass—turn upside down, when hard enough, candle will slide out;
   tin can—turn upside down, open bottom of can with *screw-type* can opener, push candle out.
   (If you want to leave the candle *inside* a glass or jar mold, you *must* use store-bought wicking with wire core or the glass may crack from the heat.)

PAPER   **GLASS**

CAN

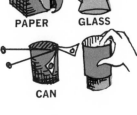

STACKED SANTA CLAUS

Read all directions on page 56. Put apron on.

Line up 3 small hot drink paper cups.

1. The amount of wax needed depends on the size of the cups. (One bar melted household paraffin fills one 4 oz. cup.) Melt 2 batches of wax; one, containing 2 bars wax, color red. Leave the other, one bar wax, plain white.

2.	Follow directions on page 56 to make wicks for each cup. Make one wick with an extra-long string on the bottom. To do this, leave a long end at the knot when tying string around penny or foil. Curl this end around on bottom of cup. Put a mark on this cup so you will know it is the one for Santa's hat.

3.	With all wicks in place, pour red wax into 2 cups (one of these is the marked cup), and pour white wax into one cup.

4.	Let wax harden all the way through, about 2 hours. To speed hardening, set cups in refrigerator. Test hardness with finger. When ready, peel paper cup off white candle and red candle with regular wick, and put marked cup aside.

5.	Remove top wickholders and cut wicks off about 1 inch from candle top. (When completed Santa is burning, you will pull up the next wick as each cup of wax burns away.)

6.	Heat frying pan on *low* fire on stove. Rub bottoms of the 2 candles on hot pan until wax begins to melt. Quickly stick melted *bottoms together*. Turn off heat under pan.

7.	Now peel paper cup off marked red candle. Cut wick off 1 inch from candle top.

8.	Reheat pan on *low* fire. Hold double candle in one hand (*white down*) and second red candle (*widest part down*) in the other. Rub candles on hot pan until wax begins to melt. Quickly stick melted *tops* together.

9.	Place Santa on a plate, *hat up*. With a pin, scratch through top of hat (this is really bottom of cup) to find the long wick. Remove this bottom wickholder and pull wick up.

10.	Stick tiny beads, sequins, or paper through pins and push into white wax to make Santa's face.

11.	Melt one bar white wax in double boiler. Remove melted wax from heat and let cool. Read directions for Whipped Wax on page 59. When wax begins to get cloudy, whip until it is foamy and will hold shape. Put a drop of whipped wax on top of hat *around* wick, give Santa a whipped beard, and he is finished.

WHIPPED CANDLE

Read all directions on page 56.

MATERIALS: 6 bars household paraffin, wicking or medium thick cotton string, bowl, egg beater or fork, frying pan, double boiler.

1. Place 2 bars wax in double boiler to melt for the whipped wax. If you want it colored, add crayons.

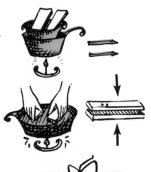

2. Heat frying pan on *low* fire on stove. Rub bottoms of 2 bars of wax on the hot pan until wax begins to melt. Quickly stick the melted sides together. Be sure they stick well.

3. Tie wicking around the *length* of the 2 bars, making a bow on top.

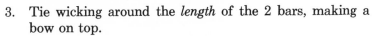

4. Holding double bar in one hand (*bow up*) and the third bar in the other hand, rub bottoms of both bars on hot pan. When wax begins to melt, quickly stick melted sides together, *covering bottom piece of string.*

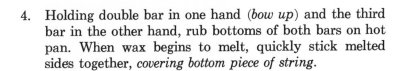

5. Holding the 3-bar candle in one hand (*bow up*) and fourth bar in the other hand, rub bottoms of both bars on hot pan. When wax begins to melt, quickly stick melted sides together.

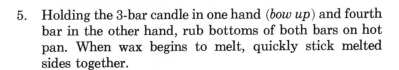

6. Untie bow. Cut wicking off 1 inch from each end of candle. You now have a wick sandwich. Stand sandwich-candle up on end on a plate or piece of wax paper.

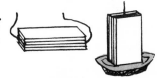

Whipped Wax:

1. Remove melted wax from heat. Let cool until wax begins to look cloudy around edges of pan. Beat with egg beater or fork until foamy.

2. When foam will hold shape, spread all over candle with fork. Do *not* cover wick. (If foam gets too stiff to spread, melt it over heat and repeat steps 1 and 2.) If you like, you can sprinkle glitter on top of candle while wax is still soft.

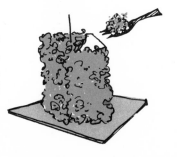

3. Clean up your utensils. Remember, hot water melts and washes away wax.

STOCKINGS

MATERIALS: Felt, wool, darning needle, straight pins, glue, pencil, scissors, lightweight cardboard.

1. Trace around the outline of this foot. (See page 11.) Tape a second piece of tracing paper onto the first at arrows (1). On that paper, draw the top of the stocking as tall as you like (2).

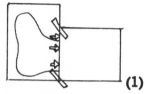 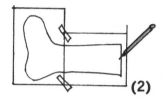

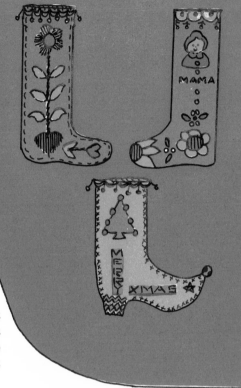

2. Transfer the pattern to cardboard. Then remove tracing paper and cut out cardboard stocking.

3. For one stocking, you need about ⅓ yard of felt 36 inches wide. Fold felt double. Be certain that the *whole* pattern fits over both layers. Hold the cardboard stocking down on the top layer of felt and draw around it. (1)

4. Remove cardboard. Pin both layers together in the center of drawing. Cut stockings out, both halves at once. (2)

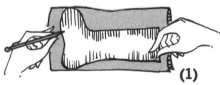 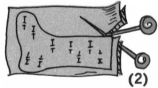 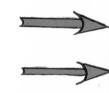

5. Before sewing stocking together, unpin and decorate the piece which will be the front of the stocking. See directions on next page.

6. *After* front half is decorated, pin it *design outside* to the back half. Read embroidery directions on next page. Thread needle with wool (same color as felt if you do not want stitches to show, different color wool if stitches are part of design). Knot one end of wool. Take first stitch from *inside* top edge of stocking to hide knot. Embroider around the sides of the pinned stocking, close to the edge. Don't forget to leave the top open! Remove pins and hang stocking on the mantlepiece for Santa to fill.

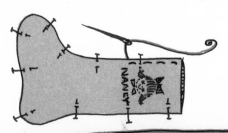

STOCKING DECORATIONS

MATERIALS: Darning needle, colored wools, tiny beads, pencil, scissors, glue, felt.

EMBROIDERY

Thread needle. Tie knot in one end of wool. Practice the following stitches on scrap cloth before embroidering stocking.

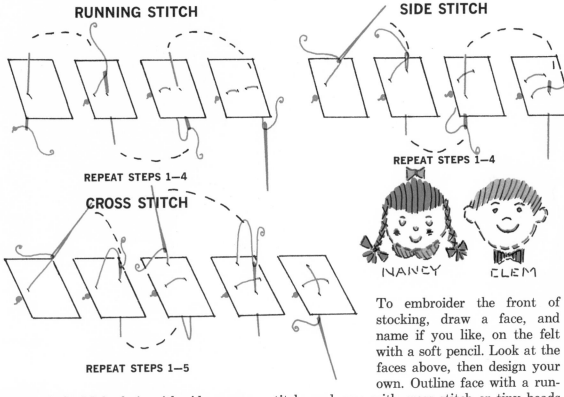

RUNNING STITCH

REPEAT STEPS 1—4

CROSS STITCH

REPEAT STEPS 1—5

SIDE STITCH

REPEAT STEPS 1—4

NANCY   CLEM

To embroider the front of stocking, draw a face, and name if you like, on the felt with a soft pencil. Look at the faces above, then design your own. Outline face with a running stitch. Make hair with side or cross stitch, and eyes with cross stitch or tiny beads sewn on. Decorate a stocking for everyone in your family.

FELT DECORATIONS

Look at faces on right, then design your own, enlarging shapes as much as necessary. Cut the pieces out of different colored bits of felt. Glue them on stocking. Trim further with braid, rickrack, or ribbon.

OLD-FASHIONED
POMANDER BALL

MATERIALS: Whole orange or lemon, box of whole cloves, sharp pencil, narrow satin or velveteen ribbon, glue, scissors.

1. Very carefully, stick the pencil point into the peel of the orange or lemon, making tiny holes close to each other all over. Don't stick in pencil too far or all the juice will run out.

2. Empty the box of cloves into a dish. Stick the stem of a clove down into each hole. Make sure the clove heads are right next to each other and the stems are pressed in.

3. Cover the fruit *entirely* with cloves. You should not see any peel showing when you are finished. If there are any bare spaces, stick in more cloves.

4. Holding the pomander ball gently in your hand, wrap a piece of ribbon around its center. Cut off any extra and glue the ends together.

5. Wrap a second piece of ribbon around the ball from top to bottom. Instead of cutting the ends, tie them into a bow. Put a tiny drop of glue *between* the ribbons where they cross (see arrow), to be sure ribbons won't slip off. Slip a piece of ribbon under the bow, pull through, and tie into a loop.

6. Hung anywhere in the house, the pomander ball has a lovely spicy scent. If you hang it in the closet, it will make your clothes smell good. It also makes a very special gift.

MISTLETOE HOLDER

MATERIALS: Lightweight cardboard—2 strips 1 inch wide by 15 inches long; glue; scissors; 2 lengths satin or velveteen ribbon—each about 1⅔ yards long by ¾ or 1 inch wide; sprig mistletoe; 2 pieces thin wire—each about 6 inches long; one piece ribbon of contrasting color—2 feet long, for bow.

1. If your cardboard is not long enough, tape two pieces together. Bend strips around into rings. Overlap ends slightly and tape well, inside and out.

2. Tape end of one length of ribbon (right side *out*) to inside of one ring. Wind ribbon over the ring, overlapping the edges as you wind.

3. Continue winding until you have covered all cardboard. Cut off any extra ribbon. To end, put drop of glue on end of ribbon and tuck it into the next loop on *inside* of ring. Pinch glued spot to secure.

4. Repeat steps 2 and 3 to make second ring. Fit one ring inside the other. The roughness of the ribbon should prevent slipping. If rings slide, put a *drop* of glue *inside* spots where rings cross.

5. Tie one piece of wire around stem of mistletoe. Hang misltetoe inside ring cage and tie other end of wire around top crossing of rings. Tie second piece of wire around top cross and up into a hanging loop.

6. Slip ribbon of contrasting color under the top crossing of rings and tie bow over the wires. Don't cover loop. If you like, add a second bow at bottom crossing of rings. Hang up mistletoe holder, stand beneath it, and have a merry, merry Christmas!

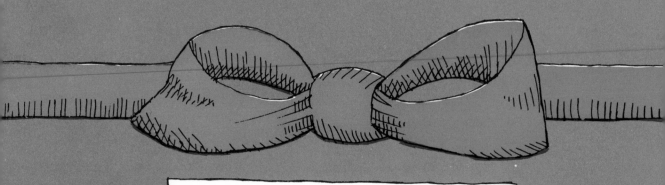

INDEX